THIS BOOK BELONGS TO

DOLLY LLAMA FINDS A WAY

To Anna + Jessica
with warm
regards to two
fellow readers—
Gail Jones

DOLLY LLAMA FINDS A WAY

by Gail S. Jones

Illustrated by Cris Hammond

GYRE & GIMBLE
PUBLISHERS
SAN RAFAEL, CALIFORNIA

The characters and events in this book are fictitious.
Any similarity to real persons, living or dead, is
coincidental and not intended by the author.

Copyright 2014 by Gail S. Jones
Gyre & Gimble, Publishers, San Rafael, California

All rights reserved. In accordance with the U. S. Copyright Act of 1976, the scanning, uploading, and electronic sharing of any part of this book without the permission of the publisher constitute unlawful piracy and theft of the author's intellectual property.

First Edition: 2014
ISBN 978-0-692-29098-9

Printed in China

Design by Yvonne Tsang

To Arthur Charles Jones,

who was mindful

of everything

CONTENTS

Dolly Makes Her Appearance *1*

Petting Zoo Pandemonium *7*

Snowstorm Under Glass *15*

Papa Llama Sits Down on the Job *22*

A Troubling Kind of Tourism *27*

No Easy Solutions *32*

Dolly Discovers Llama Sitting *37*

Mightier Than the Sword *42*

An Important Decision *47*

The Opposite of Love *50*

Dolly Finds a Way *56*

Impending Doom *61*

Adventure in the Andes *65*

Peace in the Valley *76*

Meanwhile, Back in New Hampshire *79*

Hitting the Big Time *82*

Long after Dolly Llama had become as famous as a llama can be, she continued to maintain that she was just an Ordinary Sort of Llama. Never mind that at the tender age of two, in a remote village in Peru, she had made headlines from Boston to Bangkok. Even near the end of her long and happy life, Dolly would gather her great-grandchildren around her, and put the disappointing truth to them plainly: "Any of you can do what I have done. Believe me, I'm not that special."

At this point, the sea of upturned llama faces would look so crestfallen that Dolly would hasten to add: "I may be an Ordinary Sort of Llama, but I did have one *really* extraordinary adventure!" Then a great cheer would go up, and all the little llamas would cry: "Tell us the story! Tell us the story!"

News accounts from that remarkable summer told how a herd of llamas in South America, led by Dolly Llama, captured the attention of the world. And even though you can't believe everything you read or hear, all that really was true.

But Dolly always insisted that behind the publicity her adventure received, there was another, better tale. Not a serious sermon about the meaning of life, or even a heroic tale of courage and daring. But a simple story about one young llama trying to find her own path, and how that changed everything.

Dolly Makes Her Appearance

DOLLY LLAMA was born early one cold summer morning in the mountains of Peru to Mama Llama and Papa Llama, who had waited nearly a year for her arrival. Within one hour of being born, she stood on her wobbly legs, took a few shaky steps, and tried to nurse. Baby Dolly had a soft, thick, white coat to protect her from the harsh mountain climate. She had large brown eyes, long sweeping eyelashes, and graceful banana-shaped ears. Like

all llamas, she had a curved-up mouth that always appeared to be smiling. To tell you the truth, Dolly—who was a happy little *cria*, or baby llama—usually *was* smiling.

Now, Dolly acted a lot like any young llama. But to Mama Llama, who was much Given to Drama, her first *cria* was unique in all the world. "My perfect precious! My blessed baby! My darling dolly!" she would exclaim. (Mama Llama liked to describe things in threes.) When it came to choosing a real name, however, "Precious" seemed silly, and "Baby" was hardly appropriate for a llama who already outweighed young lambs. But "Dolly" seemed just right.

Papa Llama, who was *not* Given to Drama, had reservations about her new name. "I think I've heard it before. Some kind of famous monk from Tibet," he said, wincing as Baby Dolly shrieked for milk. "You know, a learned sage who quietly ponders the meaning of the universe." Dolly wailed louder. "I'm not entirely sure the name fits," he persisted.

But Mama Llama cared little about monks or Tibet. She loved her baby's new name! "People who know this holy man might think my Dolly is also wise, wonderful, enlightened!" she exclaimed. She

DOLLY MAKES HER APPEARANCE

nuzzled her newborn, and happily hummed a bit, which is what llama parents do to calm their little *crias*.

"It's possible," Papa Llama said dubiously, eyeing his spindly-legged offspring. But as usual, he gave in to Mama Llama. He even hummed to Dolly to show Mama Llama how proud he was of his baby girl. Dolly Llama she was.

Dolly and her family lived on a ranch owned by Señor and Señora Perez in the rugged highlands of Peru in South America. The Perez family's comfortable stone and timber home had a front porch that ran the length of the house and faced the dark foothills of the Andes Mountains. By lying in a porch hammock and peering under the ancient rafters, you could see to the very top of the mountain peaks. Spreading out in a neat rectangle from one side of the house was a large, fenced pasture that contained a barn, several outbuildings, and a lively menagerie: twenty-eight llamas, thirty-two sheep, nine goats, four cats and a dog.

The Perez ranch was a destination for travelers who wanted to explore the magnificent Andes by climbing the rocky paths that wound up, up, up into

the mountains. On these treks, the Perez llamas carried all of the necessary food and equipment. They never minded this job, since adult llamas are cheerful workers and can easily carry about a quarter of their body weight—50 or 75 pounds—on their backs.

But Dolly, who was too young to help with these outings, understood little of the workaday world of Mama Llama, Papa Llama, and her older aunts, uncles and cousins. Running here and there with her llama friends, chasing stray sheep on a whim, stopping to chew some grass or sweet alfalfa—this is how Dolly spent her days, which were pleasant indeed. By the time she was a year old, she had explored every inch of the barn and pasture in which she lived, just for the thrill of seeing and feeling all there was to see and feel.

How Dolly loved life! There was never enough time in her carefree days to learn everything she was curious about. "What makes the pasture grass grow green here, but brown there?" she would ask Mama Llama. "Why does the moon disappear over the barn, then come back over the sheepfold? Why will goats eat *anything*?"

Each rosy dawn on the ranch started quietly, but as soon as the sun warmed the pasture, the barnyard chatter began. Sometimes it got very loud. When Dolly tried to outrun the noise, it only seemed to get louder. Soon it filled her ears from sunrise to sunset.

"It's like a bee buzzing in my head," she complained one day to Papa Llama. "And I can't turn it off." But each night before she dropped off to sleep, the bee would fly away, and deep inside Dolly would again feel the early morning quiet. "I wish I could keep that feeling all day long," she thought. "But how?"

Dolly found the answer that summer. It changed her life in ways she never could have imagined, ways that rocked the world far beyond her pasture playground. In fact, dear Reader, it all started with *another* little llama halfway around the world—and the human who met her.

Petting Zoo Pandemonium

CLARE CUNNINGHAM was animal crazy. At least that's what her Dad said, and with good reason. When Clare was a little girl living in Hanover, New Hampshire, her Mom and Dad gave her a tan Airedale puppy she named Cocoa. She loved that dog more than anything in the world, even when it grew to 60 pounds and knocked her over when she and her Mom wrestled with it.

Then something terrible happened: Clare's mom was killed in a car accident. Nothing her Dad could do, nothing anyone could do, filled the painful emptiness she felt inside. The only thing that made ten-year-old Clare feel better was to spend time alone in her bedroom with Cocoa. She thought more pets might make her feel even better, so she adopted a pony, a cat, an iguana, and even a pot-bellied pig. The emptiness inside never completely went away, but it helped to laugh and cry with her pets, who seemed to understand her every mood.

Clare liked to make up stories about her animals, imitating the tales she loved from her childhood: *Winnie-the-Pooh, Curious George,* and *Charlotte's Web.* She scribbled the stories in an old school notebook and shoved them under her bed, too embarrassed to show anyone. She would only read them to little kids she babysat, and was delighted to discover that they actually listened, and sometimes squealed with delight.

That was all Clare needed in the way of encouragement. "I'm going to be a writer," she announced to her Dad when she was thirteen. But writing complete stories that she thought would make sense to other people turned out to be harder than she imagined. It made it easier if the kids she babysat were her only audience, at least for now. For years, the pile of notebooks under her bed grew like mushrooms.

When Clare was eighteen, she went away to college, and made many new friends. But during visits home, she'd often find herself hanging out in the backyard shed with her animals, just like when she was little. One warm spring day, she spent an entire afternoon with her pony and her pot-bellied pig, sharing with them random thoughts about life in general. Mr. Cunningham came home from work to find chores undone and Clare apparently in deep conversation with Wilbur the pig.

Dinner was a quiet affair, with Clare wondering if she was weird. Who, really, spent hours in a barn with animals, then wrote stories about them? As if confirming her fears, Mr. Cunningham cleared his throat nervously and asked: "Clare, are you OK? You seem to be spending a lot of time out back."

Clare resented how he read her mind. "Dad, don't you know that all great authors need to find their *passion*? Well, *my* passion is animals. They are sometimes more interesting than *humans*. They *inspire* me," she said grandly.

To Clare's satisfaction, Mr. Cunningham looked mildly shocked.

"In fact, I need to broaden my horizons beyond our back yard," Clare continued. "I think I'm ready to do field research so I can learn *lots* more about animals." This thought had just occurred to her.

Mr. Cunningham smiled. "Why don't you head to the zoo? I'm sure your little cousin Abby would love to go."

Late the following afternoon, Clare found herself saddled with a cranky, sticky four-year-old who had seen too many tigers and toucans, meerkats and monkeys. But Abby insisted on one more stop: the petting zoo. Clare had always loved the baby animals, but she sometimes wondered how much *they* liked the attention from kids. Today she saw screaming toddlers grab the ears of little lambs, and older kids feeding goats their leftover lunches. Then she spied one animal standing alone by the fence: a beautiful brown and white baby llama.

Clare had never seen a llama face to face. It looked gentle and sweet, like a large toy lamb, but with a long neck and legs. The llama gazed peacefully at Clare, and seemed to smile invitingly.

Leaving Abby with the baby pigs, Clare walked up to the llama and tentatively patted its neck. The llama cocked its head to one side and stared at her. Clare stroked it more firmly and edged closer, grinning as the llama's ears began to lay back. "Just like when I scratch behind Cocoa's ears," she thought. She tickled the llama's neck harder.

Suddenly the llama shook its head and brayed "Mwaaaa!" Before Clare knew it, a chunky string of slime struck her square in the neck. It sprayed her shirt, dribbled in clumps down her jeans, and splattered her sneakers.

"Achhhh!" she screamed, dancing jerkily to shake the slime off her clothes. The whole petting zoo crowd stared and pointed, and giggles erupted here and there. Abby laughed hysterically and dropped a piglet. An attendant strolled over, frowning. "I guess I should have warned you," he said. "Llamas are herd animals and feel threatened when alone. If they get agitated, they lay their ears back. It's a warning sign. Then they spit." He glanced at Clare's sodden clothes, and grinned. "Petting zoos are *horrible* places for llamas. Guess you found out the hard way." He walked away chuckling.

Abby ran up to Clare for a hug, then stopped short. "Yuck!" she cried. "You stink!" Mortified,

Clare reached into her backpack and pulled out a plastic poncho she kept for emergencies. "Show's over, folks," she said to the staring crowd, grabbing Abby's hand. "Let's find the nearest bathroom, Abby, so I can get this disgusting shirt off. Then we're leaving." Someday, she thought, this might make a great story. But not now.

She glared at the llama one last time. "Why did you do that?" she hissed. The llama's brown eyes opened wide, and it gave a surprised gurgle. Its mouth opened and shut twice.

And then, dear Reader, it *spoke*.

"Sorry," it said.

For the second time in five minutes, Clare was dumbfounded. "Abby, did you *hear* that? I think the llama talked to me!"

"Let's *go*," Abby wailed. Everyone in the petting zoo was still laughing at her cousin, and now it seemed they were laughing at her too.

"Good-bye," Clare said softly to the little llama, who evidently had spent its single-word vocabulary and was munching grass. Clare trudged to the bathroom, put on the poncho, and dragged Abby to the car.

As Abby dozed on the way home, Clare's mind

was reeling. She *knew* the llama had spoken to her. In spite of the really gross spitting incident, she had heard it—she had *seen* it—say that one amazing word: "Sorry!"

Reader, we all know that there is a time in one's life when talking to animal friends is the most natural thing in the world, as long as one *believes* it is possible. Some people assert that llamas everywhere—in fact, most animals—can understand human speech. But for a *person* to understand *animal* speech is much, much rarer. Clare knew this, and it made her feel singled out and special.

Over the next few weeks Clare became obsessed with llamas. She checked out library books about them, and looked at articles and videos on the Internet. "Llamas are curious about everything," she told her Dad. "They're friendly and sociable and helpful to people. The zoo guy was right, they should never be kept alone in petting zoos."

"Ah, yes, the cause of the infamous spitting incident," her Dad said.

"Ha, ha," Clare responded. She was a little tired of being teased about being spat on by an animal. She certainly wasn't going to tell her Dad that the llama had *talked* to her.

Clare read that many llamas live on llama ranches in Peru, South America. There the animals are prized for their soft wool, and for their ability to guard livestock and carry burdens. She discovered to her astonishment that there are hundreds of llama farms in the United States, with many thousands of llamas roaming around on them.

But it was Peru, the llamas' native home, that really captured Clare's imagination. For centuries, llamas had lived side by side with Peruvian people as valuable members of their communities. Wouldn't it be awesome, she thought, to see llamas living among their own llama families and herds, not as adorable pets but as highly prized workers?

Clare secretly began to form a plan. She knew some Spanish. Summer was just around the corner. What if she got a job caring for llamas on a ranch in Peru? Would they like her, as her pets at home liked her? Most intriguing of all . . . would they *talk* to her? Then she'd *really* have something to write about.

Snowstorm Under Glass

Reader, would it surprise you to know that Clare did in fact brush up on her Spanish, and find summer work on a ranch in Peru? Early one June morning, Clare bid good-bye to her worried-looking Dad and her beloved pets and flew off to South America. She was brave in front of her Dad, but on the inside she admitted feeling a tiny bit scared about her new adventure.

OK, to be honest, she felt a *lot* scared.

Clare didn't need to be. Her destination—the Perez ranch, of course—was a peaceful and beautiful place, owned by the very nicest people. Like so many visitors before her, Clare would fall in love with the warm Peruvian people, and with the dramatic Andean highlands filled with fragrant grasses and dark, mysterious forests.

Deep inside these forests were cool lakes, waterfalls, and rivers, fed by the rains. For many years, the paths to these hidden places had been traveled by sure-footed llamas who could safely navigate the highest mountain passes. Though the sun rarely penetrated these remote places, it often shone with celestial splendor on the snow-capped mountaintops. This sight never failed to fascinate Dolly Llama; soon it would fascinate Clare, too.

Señor and Señora Perez were proud of their friendly herd of llamas that accompanied tourists in treks up the rocky terrain. Each summer, more and more backpackers and explorers made their way to the Perez ranch, until it seemed to Dolly that the steady stream of strangers grew larger every day.

One evening after a long day of leading people up the mountain, Papa Llama made an important announcement. "Señor and Señora Perez have hired a young girl named Clare to help us with the summer tourist season. She's a student doing research on the llamas of Peru. She wants to be a writer someday." Papa twitched his ears, scattering flies. "She seemed nice enough when she, ahem, *introduced* herself to me—in pretty good Spanish, no less." He winked at Dolly. "Then I introduced myself to *her*."

Mama Llama emitted a high-pitched laugh. "So

you had a *conversation* with this Clare? No humans understand llama speech, my dear. And if they do, they're crazy, cuckoo, coconuts!"

Now, Mama Llama was a no-nonsense sort of llama, who had never felt that humans could communicate with animals. But Papa Llama had always believed it could happen.

"I don't think Clare is crazy. I understand her Spanish, and I suspect she understands Llama. She seems to *listen* differently." Papa lifted his head in gentle defiance. "Clare told me about her life in a cold place called New Hampshire. At her home she only has a half dozen animals to take care of. And get this. Some of the llamas are in *zoos*! " He paused for this astonishing news to register.

Mama Llama predicted that no good would come of a girl who lived in such a strange place, and who pretended to understand llama speech. "That's ludicrous, laughable, loony!" she harrumphed. But eager to gossip about this new drama at the ranch, she loped off to check out the newcomer for herself.

Dolly was curious about Clare, too. Mostly, Dolly wondered whether a human might be able to understand *her*. She began to graze at the far end of the pasture by Clare's tiny cabin, hoping she would come out. Then one day Dolly noticed a shiny round object on Clare's windowsill. In the late afternoon light it looked nearly afire, and Dolly couldn't take her big brown eyes off it. She trotted up to the window, arched her neck, and peered intently into the mysterious glowing ball.

Suddenly a slender arm drew the chintz curtains wide. Clare smiled at Dolly reassuringly and held up the ball for her to see. Dolly pressed her nose to the half-moon-shaped glass, and made out a tiny village inside painted in reds and greens and yellows. "It's called a snow globe," Clare explained in Spanish. "Now, check this out."

Clare shook the globe, and a miniature snowstorm swirled around the village, hiding the tiny church spire and houses and pine trees in a turbulent eddy of white flakes. Clare and Dolly watched quietly as the snow slowly settled on the little town, and the liquid in the globe became clear again.

Dolly's nose quivered with delight. "Do it again!" she cried.

Clare's eyes opened wide. "*What* did you say?" she gasped.

"Do it again! Do it again!" cried Dolly. Clare laughed and reached through the open window to hug Dolly. "Sure thing!" she said, turning the snow globe upside down, then setting it on the windowsill for them to watch again.

Dolly felt a great surge of excitement. For the first time in her young life, a human could really *understand* her! She looked into Clare's smiling eyes and knew she had found a friend.

Soon Dolly made a habit of wandering over to Clare's window when the curtains were open, which she took as an invitation to visit. At Dolly's approach, Clare would stop scribbling in her notebook, exclaim "If it isn't my Dolly Llama!" and shake the snow globe vigorously. Dolly would gaze transfixed for many minutes at a time, watching the snowstorm settle into the crevices and corners of the village.

Clare and Dolly enjoyed the silence of snow globe gazing, but they also liked to talk. Clare would try out some of the more difficult Spanish words on Dolly, who appeared to understand them. And as Clare found she could comprehend Dolly equally well, soon every afternoon the two new friends had long conversations.

One day Clare said, "The snow globe was a gift from my mother, who died when I was ten. She used to say that when she was unhappy or upset, she would shake the globe and feel as if she could crawl inside that village, where everything was calm and beautiful."

"I think I know what your mother meant," Dolly said. "The bee in my head quits buzzing. It's like that feeling I get right before falling asleep." Clare seemed to understand, and shook the globe again. Together the two friends felt the stillness as they watched the snow fall, flake by flake, on the tiny town.

Then Dolly heard a soft hum coming from Clare.

For a moment she felt like a baby llama again, nuzzled and soothingly hummed to by her Mama Llama.

"Are you humming to *me*?" she asked Clare shyly.

Clare chuckled. "I guess I didn't realize I was doing it," she admitted. "I used to hum to Wilbur, my pot-bellied pig. I learned it from my mother, who used to hum to relax. She'd sit in one place, close her eyes, breathe in and out slowly, and hum. She said it healed her heart, made her feel calmer."

Dolly nodded happily, closed her eyes, and showed Clare how llamas hum. Clare grinned and hummed along companionably, and Dolly decided she liked pretty much everything about her new human friend.

Papa Llama Sits Down on the Job

Nearly every day in the summertime, Papa Llama would carry equipment up the mountain for hikers who wanted to visit the ruins of the ancient Inca civilization. These were long, dusty treks, but Papa Llama liked the tourists, and he enjoyed listening to their stories about life in other countries. But one morning, Papa didn't like what he saw and heard one bit.

"It was a hot morning, and I could see heat waves shimmering off the dirt road next to the barn," he told Dolly. "We were backpacked and ready for the trek, but already sweating under our loads. Señor Perez had just started talking to the hikers about camping in the mountains when this shrill voice interrupted him."

" 'I want to take my BB gun up the mountain!' "

bawled a scowling boy who stomped and shouted demands to his parents. "'And my extra ammo! And my Big Shot Slingshot!'"

"I could tell Señor Perez was embarrassed and that he wanted to let the boy's parents handle the situation. We all shuffled and whispered: 'Spoiled brat alert!' But the kid kept howling, and the tired-looking mother finally said, 'Now, Ben, be reasonable. We're *camping*. We're here to *observe* animals, not hunt them. These llamas carry only those things we'll need for our overnight trip.'"

"But Ben's caterwauling got louder, and he threw himself on the ground, kicking up clouds of dust. I sneezed up a storm and gave the kid the evil eye, but it was no use. The boy's father said, 'Well, maybe we'll bring just one or two of your toys.'"

"Señor Perez shrugged, then made a grave error. He actually slung the BB gun on my back, *and* the heavy ammo, with the kid's blasted Big Shot hung over the middle. It was *unbelievable*," Papa Llama said. "Even patient llamas like me have limits, and it was all I could do not to spit at the little bugger. But sometimes you need to Stop and Take a Stand."

Dolly nodded, eager to hear about his courageous act of defiance.

"Or rather, you need to Stop and Take what I call a Llama Sit. So I sat," Papa Llama announced proudly. "*Not* taking weapons on a nature hike seemed to be the Right Thing to Do."

"You did *what*?" asked Dolly. She thought Papa might have thrown his 250 pounds of weight around and raised a ruckus.

"I admit I was tempted to hurl a fat wad right at the kid's face. But"—Papa recollected himself—"I stopped, and I sat, and I was still. I sat through the pleading and the wheedling from the adults. I sat through the screaming from the kid. I tuned it all out. And the longer I sat, the calmer and more peaceful I felt."

PAPA LLAMA SITS DOWN ON THE JOB

"Brilliant, Papa," said Dolly. "So you did, um, *nothing*."

"Exactly. And eventually, when everyone realized they couldn't do anything to make me move, they got quiet. That's when I decided to Hum my Peaceful Hum."

Dolly stared at her Papa. "Did you say *Peaceful Hum*?" She thought of Clare's humming, and of Mama Llama humming to her as a little *cria,* and how both made her feel calm and safe.

"It was quite a moment," Papa Llama recalled, a faraway gleam in his eyes. "The parents stopped to listen. Señor and Señora Perez stopped to listen. The sheep and the goats twitched their ears to listen. That annoying kid was rendered speechless! His eyes were bugging out of his head!"

Dolly laughed, and Papa Llama warmed to his theme. "He gave it a rest! Put a sock in it! Closed his pie-hole!" Dolly roared.

"Then Señor Perez smiled and took some of the kid's stuff off my back. The brat didn't make a peep, and we started the trek in silence. You know," Papa Llama continued reflectively, "Llama Sitting and Peaceful Humming can come in handy." He glanced at Dolly. "Any llama can do it. You might want to try it sometime."

Dolly trotted away, not quite knowing what to make of Papa Llama's story. If her Papa was telling the truth (and he *always* told the truth), Llama Sitting and Peaceful Humming had turned a bad situation into a good one. It was odd how Clare often did the same thing—sitting and humming—just for herself.

Dear Reader, did you know that llamas have *three* parts to their stomachs? Like cows, they often regurgitate food from their stomachs to chew it again before it is digested. That's the origin of the phrase "chew something over."

Now, if the idea of Llama Sitting had been food, you can bet that Dolly would have reached way back to all three parts of her stomach to chew on the meaning of *that*.

A Troubling Kind of Tourism

By midsummer, the Perez ranch was a hubbub of activity. All twenty-eight llamas, thirty-two sheep, nine goats, four cats and the dog were up at the crack of dawn just to get ready for the day. Every older llama that could serve as a pack animal was put to work taking tourists up the mountain. Clare toiled long hours keeping the animals healthy and well fed. She found little time to write.

The great incoming tide of people seeking outdoor adventure didn't stop at the Perez ranch. All of the llama farms in the valley seemed busier than ever, hosting explorers from many countries who wanted to experience the beauty of the mountains.

One fine summer day Señora Perez, Señor Perez and Clare were enjoying a particularly tasty lunch of fresh corn tamales, or *humitas*. Señora Perez was

idly scanning the newspaper. Suddenly she let out an "Oh, NOOO!"

Señor Perez, who had been concentrating heavily on his food, startled and spilled lemonade on his shirt. "What's the matter?" he grunted.

"We're doomed!" she screeched.

"What in the world, Ana?" asked Señor Perez.

"The devil has returned!" cried Señora Perez dramatically. "That crazy developer with his 'Adventure in the Andes' theme park! And he's building not a mile from our ranch!" Clare's fork stopped halfway to her mouth.

"Want to hear the gruesome details?" Señora Perez wailed. "A Machu Picchu Hideaway Hotel with a Magic Energy Spa. A Lake Titicaca Water

Park, complete with floating islands. An Inca Sinka Putt mini golf course! And . . . a Llama Land with LLAMA RIDES!" She threw the paper on the floor in disgust.

"Now, Ana, maybe it won't be as bad as all that," Señor Perez said unconvincingly. He stooped to retrieve the newspaper, and spread it out on the worn kitchen table. A few minutes later he stood up, lips pressed grimly together, and began pacing the kitchen in his clumping work boots.

To Clare, his silence was worse than Señora Perez's outbursts. She tiptoed around the table and quickly read the story that was causing the uproar. A knot of fear formed in her stomach.

"So what will this do to your beautiful ranch?" she asked, surprised to hear the trembling in her own voice.

"For starters, they'll chop down the old forest at the end of the road," said Señora Perez. "Not to mention destroy the beauty of our ranch land. They'll ruin an environment for miles around that has been a home to people for centuries."

"My great-grandfather built this house, timber by timber, stone by stone," Señor Perez added. "My father was born here, and his father before that. We all raised llamas and sheep. This life—this beautiful mountain life—is all we know." His voice broke.

Señora Perez slammed a cabinet door shut, and the dog slunk out of the room. "We dealt with these people a year ago, when they were *asking our permission* to build next to our ranch," she said. "You see, we don't own the property they want to build on, but we do own the road needed to move construction equipment to their worksite. So naturally we said no. A small hotel is one thing. We would welcome that. It would give jobs to our neighbors! But we sure didn't want them using our road to build an eyesore of a tourist center."

"Now, I guess, they don't *need* our permission," Señor Perez said hollowly. "The paper said construction starts in a month. They must have more money than they had before, or more political power, and now they'll do whatever they want." He slumped in his chair. "I'll talk to my cousin, a lawyer in Cuzco, but these people are very big developers, and we—we're just ranchers." Señora Perez sat down next to him and tenderly took his hands in hers. Huddled at the table, to Clare they looked tired and defenseless.

"I can't *believe* this! We won't take this lying

down! I'll . . . I'll write them a nasty letter!" Clare cried.

Señora Perez smiled sadly. "*Muchacha,* that's great, go ahead. You are smart and kind to help us. But, my sweet one, it won't do any good."

Clare ran out of the kitchen, feeling hot tears run down her cheeks. What would happen to the Perez family now? And to her beloved llamas? If their environment were destroyed, what would become of their nature treks into the mountains? All this to build a huge theme park—with, of all things, a Llama Land. Something must be done, and quickly.

No Easy Solutions

Whenever she was upset, Clare reached for a pendant she always wore around her neck. She would feel its circular shape and remember her mother saying that as long as you have peace in your heart, everything will turn out all right.

Today, even this special necklace didn't offer much comfort. She spied Dolly and Papa Llama loping across the pasture, and wiped her eyes with the back of her hand.

One look at Clare's face, and the two llamas asked what was up. "Right next to the ranch, developers want to cut down an old forest and put in a big theme park called 'Adventure in the Andes,' with miniature golf and a water slide," Clare said dully, leaving out the part about Llama Land.

Papa Llama grimly shook his head. "Wait till

Mama Llama finds out. *Major drama,*" he predicted. Dolly blurted: "Won't this theme park ruin the mountains? Aren't the mountains what the tourists *come* for?"

"Yes, to both questions," Clare replied. "They might make a lot of money, but the valley will never be the same. A small hotel would be all right. But from what I've read, this huge theme park will be bad news. It'll wreck the environment, and permanently change the lives of the people who live here. I guess the developers can do it because they own the land, even if the Perez family owns the road that leads to it."

"But . . . what will happen to the ranch? We have to DO something!" cried Dolly. The bee in her head was buzzing like mad. "This is our HOME! We need to FIGHT!"

Dolly thought about how disagreements were settled in the pasture: a little spitting, a little neck wrestling, and everyone knew who was in charge. "If they were here right now, I'd . . . " She stomped the ground with her feet.

Papa Llama gave a long look at Dolly and Clare. "Sometimes you can do something about things you don't like, and sometimes you can't. The important thing is to know the difference. And while you can't always control a situation, you can control your reaction to it, how you handle it."

Clare nodded. "I for one intend to prove that the pen is mightier than the sword. I'm going to write them a *very* strongly worded letter," she asserted.

Papa Llama smiled fondly at Clare, but Dolly stared at her as if she were crazy. "You think a *letter* will stop them? No way! This developer will turn our mountain into a roadside attraction! It's not only wrong . . . it's . . . it's . . . EVIL!" And even though she was too grown up to act like a *cria,* Dolly threw herself on the ground and bawled.

"So you want to rid the world of evil," Papa Llama said. "OK, then. We need to have a talk."

"TALK! We need to act NOW!" Dolly screeched. She knew she sounded out of control, but the buzzing in her head positively *hurt.*

"No, we need to talk about how you make a difference in this world. You make a difference one llama at a time, and you do it peacefully," Papa Llama said.

Dolly took a deep breath. "I'd like to show these humans a thing or two," she said, glancing at Clare. "Present company excepted."

"We all want life in the mountains to go on as

it always has, with a roof over our heads, enough to eat, and a loving family," Papa Llama said. "But even those wonderful things will not be enough unless you have a peaceful mind and heart to help you through bad times. And that, Dolly Llama, is why I do this." He grunted and settled himself in his Llama Sitting position, his long legs tucked under him.

"*Really,* Papa? You've got to be kidding," Dolly said, but she smiled as she shook her head. However clueless, he *was* trying to help.

"I think I know what you mean," Clare said, sitting cross-legged next to Papa Llama. "It's important to take action, but first you have to be in the right frame of mind." Dolly looked at Clare, surprised. Was *she* wimping out, too?

"Dolly, do you remember what it feels like to watch my snow globe?" Clare asked. "Each flake is like a thought that slowly sinks from view until the sky is clear. Then your mind is clear!"

"That's a good one," said Papa Llama. "Llama Sitting is *exactly* like that. And any llama can do it."

"I still don't understand!" cried Dolly. "How can just sitting change things?"

"Llama Sitting doesn't change *things*," said Papa.

"Well, it can, but first it changes *you*. It focuses your mind on the present moment, helping you see what's really going on, without judging or reacting. Then when you decide to act, you might do so with greater insight and compassion."

"That's really beautiful," breathed Clare, feeling for her necklace.

"That's a bunch of sheep manure," Dolly muttered to herself. Aloud, she said, "OK, OK. I don't get why this helps, but I'll try. Now *how* exactly do you do this?"

Dolly Discovers Llama Sitting

"First, find a quiet place," said Papa Llama. "Then sit on the ground, like me." Dolly collapsed on the grass, giggling, and looked up expectantly.

"That's fine. Look at the ground a few feet in front of you. Now think about your breathing. Feel the air come into your nose, then feel it go out. You can count if it helps you to focus.

"Your thoughts and feelings will settle down, just like when you watch the snow globe. Let them go! Watch them drift down like snowflakes, or float away like autumn leaves. Be aware of your breathing in and out, in and out."

Dolly stared hard at the ground, clenching her teeth in concentration. She tried to ignore the steady buzz in her head. Papa Llama heard Dolly inhale and exhale loudly, muttering "four, five, six . . ."

He chuckled. "Dolly, you don't need to force your breathing. Just let it flow naturally."

Dolly breathed quietly for a few moments. Then she sputtered in exasperation: "But I keep *thinking!!*"

"Don't worry. It can take a long time to develop mindfulness. Many feelings and thoughts will come, but they are just like the waves on Lake Titicaca. If you're not bothered by the waves, they'll subside. And once you get a nice, quiet feeling, remember what that is like—and carry it with you all day long."

All was silent for two or three minutes. Then Dolly jumped up.

"But I feel like I should be DOING something!" she cried. "I'm not solving our problem—this theme park that's coming to ruin our valley!"

Papa smiled. "Do you remember that whining kid the other day, who was driving everyone nuts?" Dolly nodded. "And how my Llama Sitting and Peaceful Humming helped . . . all by 'doing' nothing?"

Dolly thought about this. "OK, I get it," she said finally. "I'll give it another shot." For awhile there was only the soft sound of breathing. Then Dolly's ears began to twitch. Her legs felt cramped. There were a half dozen places on her neck she just *had* to

scratch. She glanced up at Clare and Papa Llama, whose eyes were closed and who seemed to be far away. Then Papa opened one brown eye partway.

"If you want to," he whispered, "you can Hum. Peacefully."

Finally, something she knew how to do! Soon an off-key Hum came from Dolly's direction, and she relaxed into a pattern of smooth, regular inhaling and exhaling.

After a few more minutes, Dolly scrambled to her feet. "I feel better," she admitted. "But, Papa, I'm still mad! I *don't* trust humans. They create so many problems! And this theme park will be terrible! What can one llama do? What can *I* do?"

"Keep Llama Sitting, and Humming, and you might discover the answer on your own," said Papa Llama. "But be patient, since the solution may not come right away."

From across the pasture, they saw Mama Llama coming their way, looking upset. Clearly, the llama grapevine had reached her. "What in the world are you three *doing*? Don't you know we're in a *crisis*? I have been *incredibly* anxious about this ghastly theme park business, and have had a *most* difficult afternoon. This is *so* distressing, disturbing, discombobulating!" she wailed, her voice rising with each word.

Papa turned to Dolly. "Like I said, patience may be in order," he observed.

Mightier Than the Sword

Several days later, Dolly Llama was idly munching a tasty bit of alfalfa when she heard voices coming from the ranch house. She edged closer to the open window of the Perez kitchen to listen.

"We need to fight this 'Adventure in the Andes,'" she heard Señora Perez say. "Our parents and grandparents and great-grandparents made a life on this land. Our blood and our ancestors' blood is in this soil. We can't let it go!"

"You're a strong woman, Ana," responded Señor Perez. "But a new world is coming to change these old ways, a powerful world, stronger even than you or me." He cleared his throat. "My dear, I don't know how to tell you this, but I've spoken to my cousin Carlos, the lawyer in Cuzco. He—he won't take our case against these developers. None of his lawyer friends will, either. They're afraid of big money, big business, and the forces behind them."

From behind the window, Dolly saw Señora Perez sink into a chair and rub her forehead. Then she got up slowly and took a well-creased sheet of paper out of a bureau drawer. "Clare thinks we should talk to them, reason with them." She laughed bitterly and passed the paper to her husband. "So she wrote a lovely letter—in Spanish, no less—one that would earn an 'A' at her college. But it won't change anything."

Señor Perez adjusted his reading glasses on his broad nose, peered at the letter, and read it aloud.

For you, dear Reader, here it is in English:

I am writing to protest the "Adventure in the Andes" tourist development, proposed for the land adjoining the ranch owned by my employers and friends, the Perez family.

Surely you know why tourists seek out this beautiful corner of the planet, the fascinating country called Peru. They arrive and breathe the air of wild places, filled with the echoes of ancient civilizations. They walk on paths trod for centuries by the Incas, whose remarkable history remains mysterious to this day.

The Incas and their ancestors—including the Perez family—consecrated this land for us, and we have no right to disrespect it. Please understand I have no issue with commercial development that is sensitive to our natural environment. I am not against businesses and buildings that complement the landscape, that have no need to offer sham, silly amusements, that honor the real culture of this land and its people. In fact, thoughtful development may keep the llama trekking business alive for many years to come!

But please think before you build tourist attractions that destroy the environment and consume valuable natural resources. Think about what tourists really come for: the untouched beauty of this special place. Think about the legacy of the generations of families who loved and worked this land. Above all, think about doing what is right.

All of the tourists who have yet to visit this magic place will thank you for it. The hardworking families in the valley will thank you for it. The Perez family will thank you for it, and so will their llamas. You have my word on that.

Respectfully,
Clare Cunningham

Señor Perez blinked rapidly and passed his work-hardened hand across his eyes. "Eloquent, yes?"

"Oh, yes. But will it stop them?" queried his wife. "I think not." She shrugged, but Señor Perez noticed that she placed the letter very carefully back in the bureau drawer.

Dolly wandered away from the open window,

deep in thought. "So the Perez family wants to fight, but their hands are tied. Clare is writing beautiful letters that will go nowhere. Papa said that llamas have been here longer than any of them. We must have learned something, surviving generations of mountain living! How can *we* help humans now?"

An Important Decision

For the first time in her short life, Dolly Llama was truly scared. What would happen to her llama family, and to the Perez family, if "Adventure in the Andes" became a reality? What if the ranch went out of business, and the llama herd were sold and scattered? What if she became separated from her friends, from Señor and Señora Perez, or—most unthinkable of all—from Mama and Papa Llama? All three of Dolly's stomachs ached, and the bee in her head started buzzing again.

She remembered what Papa Llama had said about Llama Sitting, that it might help her discover a solution to the problems at the ranch. And that any llama could do it—even (Dolly thought) a very Ordinary Sort of Llama like herself.

And so, dear Reader, right then and there, feeling

she had nothing to lose, Dolly Llama made one of the most important decisions of her life. She began to practice Llama Sitting.

At first Dolly felt awkward and self-conscious. But she kept at it. She practiced when she woke up in the morning. She practiced after lunch, when the other llamas were cavorting around the pasture. (She tried to ignore the curious stares of her llama friends.) She practiced right before bed, when she normally played hide-and-seek.

Dolly eagerly awaited the results of her efforts. After all, she was trying so hard, like cramming for a test in school. Maybe, she thought, the solution to the problems at the ranch would magically appear! She imagined a ghostly spirit emerging from the mountain mists, dispensing words of wisdom to one and all.

But nothing happened.

After four days of Llama Sitting practice, Dolly was beginning to feel like it was a waste of time. Nobody and nothing showed up to tell her what to do.

"I *must* be doing Llama Sitting wrong," she complained to Papa Llama.

He just chuckled. "The answers will come from

AN IMPORTANT DECISION

inside of you, Dolly. You know what it's like to be in a dream, right?" Dolly nodded. "Well, Llama Sitting is a bit like waking up from a dream and seeing reality for the first time. Seeing not what you *think* is happening, but what is really right in front of you. Don't worry. You *can't* do it wrong!"

So Dolly kept Llama Sitting. Occasionally she hummed her Peaceful Hum at the same time. And little by little, she started to relax during her Llama Sits. As she learned how to push aside her worries, the buzzing in her head got quieter. For the first time, she felt she was *choosing* what she wanted to think about.

Dolly still didn't have an answer to the problems facing the ranch, but she had more hope that one might come along. She couldn't explain it to herself, but she felt different. More alive and awake and aware. Whatever had happened to her, it felt good.

The Opposite of Love

It was a pristine morning in the Andes highlands. The sky was clear and bright, and when Dolly stepped out of the barn, she felt the cool air riffle her fur and tickle her nose. For no reason at all, she felt a surge of happiness—until she heard loud, angry voices coming from the ranch house porch. She crept closer, and saw Clare and Señor and Señora Perez talking to a group of workmen.

"We got your letter, with all your fancy language," snarled a man who seemed to be in charge. "Lady, you need to save the planet on your own time." His brawny hand slapped the timber porch rail. "The owner couldn't come today. He said he wasn't going to waste his time on one rancher's crackpot complaints."

Señor and Señora Perez looked stricken, and he softened his tone. "I'm sure you have your reasons for hating what's in the works. But the developers have crunched the numbers. This project is a go. My crew's here to check out the worksite, and we have orders to move forward *now*. Millions of dollars are at stake. So if tourists want to come here to get in touch with nature, we'll make sure they can. Right, men?"

Dolly heard a chorus of approving grunts.

"Let me get this straight, Mr. Wilton," Clare said evenly. "Your boss wants to build a tourist destination that clutters up the natural landscape with huge ugly buildings and unnecessary amusements, while destroying our serenity in the process."

"Look, lady," Mr. Wilton sighed. "I've got a signed contract to do the work, and frankly, ugliness is a matter of opinion. I kinda like water slides and mini golf myself. And besides, what would my kids do in a godforsaken place like this? Ride those llamas into the ground?"

"I wouldn't let your children within a foot of my llamas," Señora Perez muttered in a dangerously quiet voice.

Clare's tone sharpened. "Surely there must be a way to build a hotel that blends into the landscape and complements the natural environment?"

Mr. Wilton snorted. "Look, I'm just doing my

job. People like me around here *need* jobs, and you're worried about what this place *looks* like? Listen. The owner has big plans that will give people a big return on their investment." He turned to Señora Perez. "I'm just tryin' to be nice here. This isn't your land, and we don't need your permission. We just got to use your road, is all. If these developers wanted to build the Leaning Tower of Pisa, I'd help as long as I got paid."

"What you are doing is *wrong!*" Clare cried harshly. She looked intently from one man's face to the next.

"Why do you want to build fake Peru attractions when the real Peru is so magical already? Don't you care about the beauty of these mountains? Do you really think you can *improve* on them?" Clare stared furiously at a sullen-looking man who avoided her eyes. She moved on. "How about you?" she asked a young worker, who shrugged and spit out of the side of his mouth. "Or you?"

Clare's voice quavered, but she pleaded her case, man by man, to an audience of mute stares. Finally, there was no one left to ask.

"Sorry, little lady, but it looks like you're alone here," Mr. Wilton smirked.

Señora Perez rushed over to hug Clare. "Get

off my property!" she cried to the group of men. The foreman shook his head in disgust. "Now!" she screamed. Mr. Wilton motioned to his crew, and they noisily stomped off the verandah.

Handing Clare a handkerchief, Señora Perez said reassuringly, "That Mr. Wilton brought his whole crew here just to scare us. But they didn't, did they? We'll figure out something, *muchacha*."

"But I thought a civil letter, and an honest conversation, would do some *good*," Clare said. She hugged Señora Perez, trudged down the porch steps, and almost tripped over Dolly. At the sight of Dolly's sad brown eyes, she broke down again.

"I just don't understand!" Clare buried her face in Dolly's soft fur. "How can these people destroy this place? There's ancient history here. I *love* these mountains!"

Taking a few deep, shuddering breaths, Clare felt for her necklace, her talisman in times of stress. "My mom once told me what the opposite of love is," she said. "It's not hate. It's *apathy*. It's knowing you need to pay attention, but ignoring a problem anyway. It's being able to right a wrong, and doing nothing."

Clare smiled ruefully. "Mom thought that peace and love would solve everything. In the sixties she and her friends would sometimes participate in a sit-in." Seeing Dolly's confused look, she explained, "That's a peaceful demonstration of a belief in something important."

Dolly thought about what she knew of peace and love. Certainly, Mama and Papa Llama had always shown her love . . . in most cases, just by listening and making sure she was OK. That, she thought, was the opposite of apathy.

"I love this ranch too," Dolly said. "These mountains are my home. It just never occurred to me that they *belonged* to anyone, or that I could *lose* them."

Dolly suddenly realized that the solid world of her childhood was, in fact, very fragile. It could be changed forever if humans were allowed to Do the Wrong Thing. She knew in her heart that Clare's mother had been right to stand up for what she believed in. And she knew, too, that the kind of change proposed by Mr. Wilton's boss needed to be stopped.

Attention would need to be paid. By somebody. Maybe, just maybe, by some *llama*.

Dolly Finds a Way

Over the next few days Dolly watched Papa Llama silently worry about what he called the Impending Doom, the coming of the theme park. She watched Clare, who read the papers and knew every depressing detail about the bulldozers, tree pullers, backhoes, and construction workers that would soon descend on their idyllic home. She watched Mama Llama, who for once had little to say, except that the proposed development would bring much trouble, trial, and tribulation.

Clear-cutting of the forest at the end of the road—the first step in construction—was a mere three weeks away.

"I've thought and I've thought, but there's not a lot more we can do," Clare moaned to Dolly. "The Perez family has held meetings with everyone on the Cuzco municipal council. I've written more letters.

I've talked to the landowners, to city government, to everyone. We can't change the developers' minds, and we can't seem to stop them. I'm so frustrated! All I can do is sit and do nothing!"

Dolly wandered away, Clare's last words echoing in her head: "All I can do is sit and do nothing!"

The next morning, as soon as the sun cleared the mountain tops and spread its warmth over the grass, Dolly began gathering small groups of llamas together. She talked earnestly to them, punctuating her comments by drawing strange patterns in the dirt with her feet.

From her cottage Clare heard loud animal chatter, and saw much sitting down and standing up. She chuckled to herself and left Dolly alone. "Dolly is really taking this to heart," she thought. "Whatever she's doing, it's a harmless distraction for her now."

Little did she know that Dolly was on a mission that would take every ounce of her young energy and resolve, and involve every single animal on the Perez ranch.

Dolly Llama no longer played, carefree and laughing, in the pasture. Every precious hour of daylight was spent laying the groundwork for her grand plan.

Toward the end of each day Dolly could be seen Llama Sitting, alone, at the far end of the enclosure. Then she'd fall asleep exhausted in the barn.

Papa Llama watched Dolly, smiled to himself, and said nothing.

The Impending Doom was only five days away when it occurred to Dolly that she might ask the sheep on the ranch to help. Handling the matter would require tact. As everyone knows, llamas often herd sheep—and Dolly for one never knew if the sheep took this personally.

The curmudgeonly Colonel Avery had been the sheep herd's leader for as long as Dolly could remember. Carefully timing her request at the best time of day—right after the sheeps' breakfast—Dolly explained the urgency of the situation to the ram. She ended dramatically: "So, what we're really doing is fighting something that's bad for the ranch, bad for the environment, bad for the Perez family, and bad for us!"

Avery fixed Dolly with a sour stare. "You llamas have pushed us around for years now. Why should we help *you*?"

Dolly's heart sank. "Don't you see, we're all in this together! If our little corner of these mountains is made into a tourist center, we *all* suffer the consequences! The ranch might be sold, and the sheep and llama families scattered. We might never see each other again!"

"You llamas are big animals, the kings of this ranch! Why don't you throw your weight around and get tough?" Avery whined.

"Because the workers might try to fight force with force," said Dolly. "No, we must do something peaceful. Clare gave me the idea, though she didn't know it at the time. One llama, one sheep, peaceably Doing the Right Thing would be great, but it might not stop them. A whole herd of llamas, and a whole herd of sheep, all peaceably Doing the Right Thing, would be a different story."

Remarkable, Avery thought. And here I thought she was a flighty little flibbertigibbet. She's defi-

nitely her father's child—with a bit of Mama Drama thrown in.

Out loud, he said, "Fine, fine. Just remember one thing: you owe me *big time* for this, Dolly. Especially when it comes to herding us during shearing season. Now, no more of your chatter! Tell me exactly what you want us sheep to do."

Dolly let out a squeal and scampered around the elderly ram. "Colonel Avery, you're the best!" she cried, and excitedly sketched out her grand plan. To Dolly's great satisfaction, the ram nodded resignedly and ambled away to hold a conference with his flock.

Dolly heaved a sigh of relief. To tell the truth, she had sounded more confident with Colonel Avery than she felt. In moments of doubt, she wondered what an Ordinary Sort of Llama like herself was doing sticking her curious nose in things she might not understand. She still had so much to figure out about Doing the Right Thing on the big day! But now she had Colonel Avery on her side, and that felt very, very good.

Impending Doom

As the ominous day approached to break ground for "Adventure in the Andes," Clare became more and more listless. Where once she had approached her daily tasks with gusto, now she plodded through her work routine. Her letters to city leaders, while politely acknowledged, hadn't done a thing to delay plans for the development. Still, in her letters to her Dad in New Hampshire, Clare said that everything was fine. Her Dad already thought she was crazy, going all the way to Peru to take care of a herd of llamas. What if he knew about the danger of the Impending Doom?

On the evening before construction was to begin, a weary-looking Dolly shambled up to Clare's cottage. Noticing that the curtains were closed, she head-butted the wood door. When Clare finally opened it, she looked at Dolly through swollen, red eyes.

"I've come to tell you something," Dolly said.

Clare smiled weakly. "Oh, Dolly, I've seen you playing in the pasture, and I'm glad you've found some new games to amuse yourself with. But those little games will need to stop tomorrow when the big plans get underway."

"Actually, that's when my work will begin for real," said Dolly. "Those little games, as you call them, are *my* big plans."

"I think you'd better tell me what's up," Clare said.

"I've been wanting to do that for ages," sighed Dolly. "This *had* to be a secret from Señor and Señora Perez. I didn't know if they'd go along with my plans. And since you work for them, I had to keep them a secret from you, too. Believe me, I wanted your help. You're my best friend. But now everything's in place, and I—I'm scared." Dolly's eyes welled up with tears. "I really need you to tell me that I am Doing the Right Thing."

Clare reached out and drew Dolly inside. For the next several hours, the two friends talked in low tones in the comfort of the cozy cottage. Oc-

IMPENDING DOOM

casionally a gasp or a giggle punctuated the murmur of conversation. In the nearby barn, Avery opened his eyes, cocking his ears to hear something that sounded like humming. He shook his grizzled head. Things are getting pretty strange around here, he thought, then fell back asleep.

Huddled over her mug of tea, one arm draped around Dolly's neck, Clare liked what she heard. The feeling was so good, it was as if her mom were there in the room with them, inspiring and guiding them both. And as Dolly listened to her friend's words of encouragement, she too felt real hope for the first time in many weeks.

It was close to midnight before Dolly crept out of Clare's cottage and nestled into her small corner of the stable. But once in her bed, Dolly felt the serenity of the cottage drain away. She tossed and turned and burrowed deeper in the straw. Eventually she fell asleep dreaming she was safe inside a snow globe village where nothing, absolutely nothing, could disturb the peace.

Adventure in the Andes

Dolly awoke in the semi-dark of early morning, remembering anxious dreams about monstrous earth-moving machinery that snapped trees like twigs with a sickening splintering sound. Taking a deep breath, Dolly inhaled the familiar childhood smells of the barn—a comforting mixture of sweet alfalfa, sheep, and Mama Llama's soft coat. Now that the day of reckoning had arrived, Dolly wished she could bury herself in the straw and ignore the plans she had set in motion only weeks before. Plans that now, in the warmth and security of the barn, seemed fraught with danger.

Feeling the old, familiar buzzing in her head, she sighed and forced her stiff legs up. A weak shaft of morning light shone through a crack in the weathered timber, illuminating the sleeping llamas. Dolly approached each huddled group and whispered: "Time to get up!"

She craned her long neck over the sleeping forms of Mama and Papa Llama. "This is the big day!" she said. "Can you follow me, *please?*" Papa Llama opened one sleepy eye and gave her a knowing wink. Mama Llama, who had never seen Dolly awake so early, scrambled quickly to her feet. "I *knew* my little Dolly was up to something strange, secret, surreptitious!" she exclaimed.

"Please, Mama and Papa, trust me! We have important work to do this morning. I've organized a kind of . . ."

Mama sputtered. "Dolly Llama, *now* what have you done? This is the limit, the last straw, the living end! There's no way—"

"Mama!" Papa's firm tones rang out in the quiet barn. "Now is *NOT* the time for drama!"

Mama Llama gasped and stared intently at Dolly, who stared back at her pleadingly. Papa Llama grinned at Dolly. "Now is the time for *ACTION!*" he said, and playfully nudged Mama Llama, who smiled half-heartedly. Maybe my little Dolly is growing up, she mused, thoughtfully trailing Papa Llama out of the barn.

With Papa and Mama Llama unexpectedly taking the lead, amid many grumblings all twenty-eight llamas on the Perez ranch—young and old, lively and infirm—shuffled through the barn door. They made their way slowly to the far end of the enclosure.

Dolly noted with relief that Clare had delivered on her promise to unlock the pasture gate. Sure-footed even in the semi-dark, the llamas headed for the path that would take them through the grasslands to the main road. Dolly could hear muffled sounds coming from the sheepfold, with an occasional "rise and shine!" in Colonel Avery's gruff tones. Soon the sheep were following the herd of llamas down the path.

This morning, there was none of the usual banter between the llamas and the sheep. In the dawn quiet, the animals' feet struck the dry path loudly. Dolly was acutely aware of every movement and rustle in the bushes. She shivered in the chilly morning air, less from the cold than from the adventure that awaited.

Soon Dolly could see the intersection of their footpath with the main road. Each pair of animal ears swiveled this way and that, discerning a faint but unmistakable hum of motors. With each passing minute, the sound grew louder.

"Hurry! Hurry! We don't have much time!" Dolly cried, and the phrase echoed from llama to llama, and sheep to sheep. "Hurry! Hurry!" They all quickened their pace, and the sound of marching became a drumbeat of purpose and strength. The distant rumble of motors crescendoed into the heavier grinding of powerful engines.

Finally the llamas and sheep reached the crossroad. "Get in formation!" Dolly shouted. "Remember how we practiced!"

As if they had done the maneuver all their lives, the llamas shuffled to form a large circle in the intersection. Standing nose to tail, they created a solid barricade at all four points of entry. The sheep, under the direction of Colonel Avery, needed a bit more guidance, since each one tended to follow the one in front. But gradually Avery nosed all the rams, ewes and lambs into a line pattern crisscrossing the inside of the circle . . . the same pattern that Dolly had drawn over and over on the pasture grounds.

The moment had arrived. Dolly turned around to face the group.

"Listen, everybody!" Her young voice rang out clearly. "These drivers will want to use their machines to break through our barricade! But we must be strong, stronger than we've ever been before. So, how are we going to STOP them?"

"LLAMA SITTING!" bleated all twenty-eight llamas and thirty-two sheep.

Then together, as if on cue, all twenty-eight llamas sat. The sheep, at a nod from Colonel Avery, followed suit.

And none too soon! The clanking of heavy machinery grew deafening, and the first yellow bulldozer crested the hill. A second surfaced on the horizon, then another. Dolly had never seen so much big equipment or heard so much racket in her life. A glance behind her revealed many llamas with their ears laid back—a sure sign they were upset. But thank goodness, every single llama and sheep was still sitting in place.

She turned to face them one more time. "Stay in position!" she shouted. "Don't let them scare you!" Dolly was relieved to see the llamas sit up straighter and look more determined. The sheep eyed each other nervously, but steadfastly held their ground. A grim-looking Papa Llama and

Mama Llama had positioned themselves right up front.

The line of massive earth-moving equipment got longer and longer, and drew closer and closer. The deafening noise assaulted the twenty-eight pair of llama ears, and the normally placid sheep jostled each other, spooked by the strange sounds. Suddenly the driver of the lead vehicle let out a tremendous yell.

A terrific grinding of gears and screeching of brakes threw up clouds of dust as the machinery loomed huge in the frightened eyes of the animals. "MOVE!" screamed the driver, gesturing wildly. Finally, the lead bulldozer began shuddering to a stop. Closer and closer it came, until it was all Dolly could see, though she was trembling so hard everything seemed blurry. The bulldozer finally came to rest at the very front of the barricade—the length of a hay bale from Dolly's nose.

Dolly could feel the heat from the engines on her fur, and smell the acrid diesel exhaust. As she expected, the man in overalls was none other than Mr. Wilton. He looked crazy angry. She sensed a collective wave of fear pass through the animals behind her. Papa Llama and Mama Llama cast worried looks in her direction, but they remained where they were, rooted like trees.

Dolly swallowed hard and wondered for the millionth time if she was Doing the Right Thing. What if she had put herself, her family and her friends into terrible danger? What if these drivers decided after all to plow their gigantic machines through her carefully constructed barricade? Worst of all, what if she totally failed to stop the development . . . and all her preparation and protest never made any difference to anyone?

Dolly had no answers to these questions. She did, however, know one thing she could do right at this moment, when it mattered most.

She could Llama Sit like she had never Llama Sat before.

Just as she had practiced, Dolly breathed slowly and calmly as the red-faced Mr. Wilton scrambled down from the bulldozer. She breathed slowly and calmly as he strode up and thrust his angry face into hers. "What's going on here? Move out, NOW!" he barked. "And what am I doing, talking to a LLAMA?"

Some of his spittle flew into her face, but Dolly resolutely stared straight ahead, concentrating on breathing in and out, in and out. Mr. Wilton

shook his fist inches from her nose. Just when Dolly thought she might cry, he stormed around the edge of the llama circle, kicking dirt on their fur and shouting to no one.

In desperation, Dolly started her Peaceful Hum—softly at first, then more loudly to drown out the terrible buzzing in her head. Mama Llama whispered triumphantly to Papa Llama: "*NOW* is the time for drama!" and then joined Dolly with a braying Hum. Soon all the llamas had raised their voices in a collective, energetic hymn to peaceful resistance.

Behind her, Dolly could feel the vibration of all of the Peaceful Hums coursing through her small body, giving her strength, opening herself up to trust that what she was doing was right. She relaxed, held her head higher, and hummed louder.

Mr. Wilton clapped his hands over his ears. "STOP! STOP! Are these crazy animals *trying* to drive me nuts? Why can't someone tell me what's going on?"

Out of the corner of her eye, Dolly spied a girl running through the forest in a brightly colored tee shirt, her shiny silver necklace bobbing as she ran.

Behind her trailed two dark-haired people struggling to keep up.

"Wait! I'm the llama caretaker!" Clare shouted breathlessly. "Oh, it's you! Mr. Wilton!"

"You'd better explain what's going on and herd these llamas out of my way!" he demanded. "We have a job to do!"

Clare stopped short in front of the foreman. "I'm afraid I can't. This is private property, and you're trespassing," she declared.

Mr. Wilton looked ready to explode. But before he could resume shouting, Señor and Señora Perez caught up to Clare, panting and placing their hands on their knees to hold themselves upright.

"Well, well, if it isn't the stubborn ranchers!" the foreman sneered.

"Mr. Wilton!" Señora Perez managed to say between gasps. "I have one thing to say to you this morning. This is *our* road . . . and you *do not* have permission to use it!"

"*Señora,* herd these llamas out of here, now! We're scheduled to break ground today two hundred yards down that way," the man snarled, pointing his thick finger up the road.

"No, *Señor,* I will *not* do that," responded Señora

Perez calmly. "I won't allow you to build here, to destroy our ranch and our valley. And besides,"—she grinned at Clare—"have you ever tried to move twenty-eight two-hundred-fifty-pound sitting llamas?"

"I'll *MAKE* your llamas move!" screamed the foreman. "You think these bulldozers can't plow through a few measly animals?" He laughed maniacally.

"You may not want to start your development by killing animals," Señor Perez said quietly. "That wouldn't be very good publicity, now, would it?"

Mr. Wilton angrily punched numbers into a cell phone. "You'll never get away with this," he growled.

"Don't be so sure," said Clare, looking up at the sky. "I called the local TV station this morning. Looks like we have company."

Peace in the Valley

THE HELICOPTER CIRCLED THE SKY above the Perez ranch like a gigantic raucous crow. Nate, a journalist from nearby Cuzco, stared out of the whirlybird's window at the ground below. He peered at the entrance to the ranch road, rubbed his eyes, and grabbed his binoculars. A tip had reached his newsroom that strange happenings were going on here, but the sight that awaited him was beyond his expectations.

"Hey, Jose, check this out." The pilot glanced down and saw what appeared to be llamas and sheep huddled together in an intersection. A long line of motionless bulldozers and backhoes snaked along the road behind the huge knot of animals.

"Let's take her down," Jose said.

The whirlybird tilted and swooped until it hovered only a hundred feet above the herd of animals. In spite of the wind and noise, the sheep and llamas

didn't seem afraid, and gazed up at the copter with a placid curiosity. Nate passed the binoculars to Jose.

"Take a look. You won't believe this one."

Jose squinted through the binoculars, shook his head, squinted again, and blinked. Nate said: "Tell me there aren't about sixty llamas and sheep. Tell me they aren't all sitting in a perfect circle at that fork in the road, deliberately blocking all that construction equipment."

"Uh, Nate? They're *not* sitting in a perfect circle,"

said Jose in an odd voice. "See those lines crossing the circle? *They're . . . they're sitting in the shape of a peace sign.*"

Nate looked hard at the ground, then hard at Jose. "Maybe somebody herded them into that position," he said uncertainly, starting to take a video.

"They wouldn't stay like that," said Jose. "They look glued to the ground. They must have organized themselves, as a peaceful protest." He laughed loonily. "It's a sit-in!"

"Yeah, right. And I'm Doctor Dolittle."

"Look for yourself, wise guy."

Nate peered again through the binoculars. A blonde girl and two other people had joined the scene. "Jose, nobody's gonna believe this. I don't believe it myself. Wait till this hits the Web—and the papers and TV! I'm going to record this before everybody thinks we're crazy." Nate quickly shot a dozen photos, and emailed them with the video to his editor.

As so it was, dear Reader, that before an hour had passed, the world had its first glimpse of what one small herd of llamas and sheep can achieve when they Do the Right Thing.

Meanwhile, Back in New Hampshire

Mr. Cunningham woke as he woke every morning, with furry Felix curled up on his chest, staring at him intently. As soon as Mr. Cunningham stretched and yawned, Felix started a mew and cry that roused the entire household zoo.

"All right already!" Mr. Cunningham grumbled, getting out of bed gingerly to avoid entangling with Cocoa, the old Airedale terrier, who slept on the floor beside him. On his way to the kitchen he shouted "Morning, sunshine!" to Ignatius the iguana, who as usual responded with a mute, sleepy stare.

Clare had been in Peru for only two and a half months, but to Mr. Cunningham it seemed like forever. Glumly he poured himself a cup of coffee, first stepping around Wilbur, the pot-bellied pig, who had taken up permanent residence in the kitchen.

After scooping out chow for Cocoa, kibble for Felix and ground corn for Wilbur, Mr. Cunningham plopped in a chair and opened his laptop. Out of habit, to start his day he clicked on YouTube's Most Viewed video.

Mr. Cunningham snapped awake.

The video started with the droning of a helicopter, and shaky footage of construction equipment stopped on a forest road. As the chopper got closer, Mr. Cunningham was amazed to see herds of llamas and sheep blocking the bulldozers and backhoes. Strangely, the animals were sitting very still, and there were *lots* of them. Weirdest of all, they were sitting in some kind of *pattern*.

"Yeah, right. And I'm Doctor Dolittle," a voice said, and the copter swung down for a final pan of the scene. A blonde girl and two black-haired adults ran up waving their arms in front of a large hard-hatted man. Mr. Cunningham pushed his glasses up his nose and peered closely at the screen. Could it really be?

Abruptly, the video ended.

Mr. Cunningham played it five times. There was no mistake.

He blew a kiss at a framed picture of a woman

wearing a silver necklace, who looked a lot like Clare. He whooped and danced a jig around the table. "The apple doesn't fall far from the tree, does it, Wilbur?" he crowed.

Mr. Cunningham slammed open the screen door and ran to the barn to share the news with Mr. Ed, who nuzzled him in greeting. He babbled excitedly to the horse as he threw buckets of grain in the trough. Mr. Ed pawed the ground, swished his tail, and shook his head from side to side, whinnying.

What an amazing thing, Mr. Cunningham thought. Heck, what an amazing *daughter*.

Hitting the Big Time

A LIMA TV STATION had sent novice reporter Luis Condor to handle the interview at the Perez ranch. Luis had viewed the sensational video before setting out for the homestead. He privately suspected that the cockamamie scene had been concocted by some crazy blogger into a hoax YouTube video. No story here, he thought. Piece of cake.

Driving up the lane to the ranch, he saw no sign of the herds of animals from the video, and his suspicions were confirmed. Luis pulled up next to the Perez home, sending up clouds of dust, and strode to the patio where people and llamas alike seemed to be expecting him. He quickly introduced himself to Señor and Señora Perez, then got out his tablet in a no-nonsense manner.

But five minutes into the interview, the young journalist's confidence was shaken. "Let's go over this again. Now, I know about the 'Adventure in the Andes' development. But you're telling me the llamas decided to *protest* it on their *own*? That they had *opinions* about it? And you had nothing to do with it?" he asked.

Señor and Señora Perez nodded. A smiling Clare sat next to them in a hammock, her arm slung around Dolly's neck. Papa and Mama Llama listened from a corner of the porch. Close by, Colonel Avery pretended to munch on grass, but his twitching ears gave him away.

"That's right," Clare piped up cheerfully. "Dolly here recruited every llama and sheep on the ranch to help. You see, she didn't like the idea of a tourist development any more than we did."

Luis stared hard at Clare. "And this llama here—*Dolly Llama*, is it?—*told* you this."

"Absolutely," Clare affirmed. "But not until a few hours before it happened, when I couldn't do anything to stop it, even if I had wanted to—which I didn't. You see, all the *people* on this ranch never really believed we could prevent this horrible theme park from being built. But the *animals*—especially Dolly—thought differently."

"Sure she did," said the reporter.

Señora Perez added: "According to Clare, who can communicate with our llamas, Dolly knew we owned the road the developers needed to use. And Dolly felt something must be done."

Mama Llama suddenly strolled up to Clare and murmured in her ear. Clare said, "Mama Llama wants me to tell you that Dolly Llama—whom she named after a wise man from Tibet—is very intelligent, inspired, and ingenious!"

As Luis rubbed his forehead, Dolly beamed and tried hard to look brilliant. She knew she was just one Ordinary Sort of Llama, but things *had* come off rather well.

"Of course, Dolly's Llama Sitting practice helped her focus, and Find a Way," Clare added offhandedly.

"Llama Sitting?" the reporter goggled.

"Oh, yes. Papa Llama showed Dolly how to develop mindfulness." From his corner Papa Llama nodded, and an affirming bleat escaped from Avery. "So often, you know, Llama Sitting and Peaceful Humming help you pay attention to what's going on, discover the Right Thing to Do," Clare continued. She looked jubilant, as if she had enough material now for a dozen best-selling novels. "When the news of the development broke, Dolly thought that if she got all the llamas and sheep to Llama Sit in a spirit of peaceful resistance, that in itself would be the Right Thing to Do."

"Naturally," the reporter croaked.

Señora Perez grinned. "And since I don't hear any backhoes starting up, I guess it *was* the Right Thing to Do," she said pointedly.

Luis took a deep breath. He felt silly talking to a llama, but it had been a crazy day. "And I suppose you were the ringleader here?" He smiled at Dolly. "The one who got all these animals to participate in a sit-in? You know, of course, that people all over the world have seen you and your animal friends stage the world's most unusual publicity stunt. Because of you, the development you hated so much is on hold."

A great cheer rose from Señor and Señora Perez and Clare. Mama Llama, Papa Llama, and Colonel Avery bleated with joy. They all looked at Dolly, who felt a rush of happiness. So she was famous! But somehow . . . she didn't *feel* famous. In fact, Dolly wished she could tell this reporter how very Ordinary she felt. Despite being so proud of what all the llamas and sheep had accomplished, she knew any animal or person could have stood up for what was right.

But maybe, just maybe, she could *show* the reporter something. So Dolly Llama walked slowly up to him and arched her long, graceful neck inches from his thick glasses.

It was then that he saw it. Nestled in Dolly's thick white fur was a silver chain. And dangling from the silver chain was a shiny silver peace sign.

"I've seen everything now," Luis muttered. "Pretty soon someone's going to hop out from behind a tree and shout 'April Fools!' " His eyes darted furtively right and left. "But I *did* see Nate's photos, and these animals *were* sitting in the shape of a peace sign, and I don't *think* I'm dreaming."

The reporter looked into the radiant faces of Señor and Señora Perez, Dolly, and Clare. Grinning to himself, he shook his head and reached for his camera. "And on the off-chance that I'm awake and not completely crazy, I'd better get a photo of this little llama."

Now, if you look closely at llamas, it may seem as if they're smiling all the time—an inscrutable smile, like the Mona Lisa. But what Dolly gave the reporter at this moment was an intentional, super-blissful smile—the smile of a llama who has Found a Way.

And that, dear Reader, was the smile seen round the world.

ACKNOWLEDGMENTS

Heartfelt thanks to my daughter Lauren Simpson, who always believed in this book; to astute readers Eric Nelson, Felicia Crosby and Carolyn Jones Filak, whose advice informed the story to no small degree; to Chris Loker, for her warm friendship and support; to Barbara Burke, spiritual advisor and friend; to illustrator Cris Hammond and book designer Yvonne Tsang, who made Dolly come alive on the page; and to David Pettus, whose love makes everything possible.